Running Presentations & Meetings

Guide on How to Improve Communication Skills in Front of Your Co-Workers, Boss and Clients

medical or professional advice. The content within this book has been derived from various sources. Please consult a licensed professional before attempting any techniques outlined in this book.

By reading this document, the reader agrees that under no circumstances is the author responsible for any losses, direct or indirect, which are incurred as a result of the use of information contained within this document, including, but not limited to, — errors, omissions, or inaccuracies.

Table of Contents

Introduction

The primary purpose of any business is to sell. In business, you're either selling a product, a concept, or a topic. Your knowledge of the content you want to sell is the most important asset you have at your disposal when making a business presentation. It is highly likely that your audience will not be comfortable with buying what you are selling if you know only a few things about what you are selling.

In 2017, a presentation software company, Shufflrr, conducted research on the behavior of 1,500 US-based professionals in business presentations, and the results were grim. Twenty-five percent admitted having fallen asleep because they were so uninterested with the material, one out every 12 claimed to have been unengaged and solely focused on browsing a dating app, and one out of every 25 people said they walked out of presentations that went on for too long.

When delivering presentations to your colleagues, the senior management of your company, a venture capitalist, or even a general audience, a successful presentation is not just about the colorful slides you create, it's way more than that.

Businesses are losing time, money, and opportunities due to the poor presentation skills of their representatives. A lousy presentation can make small business owners and entrepreneurs lose investors and big clients, while a strong presentation can single out a business from its competitors.

What differentiates strong presentations from bad ones comes down to the contents of this book. This book will give you insights into the steps to take to prepare for an effective business presentation in which your audience is engaged and interested, from knowing how to handle the presentation tools, to the kind of dress to wear, the right attitude to have during the presentation, keeping to time, and establishing credibility with business colleagues, associates and clients.

The business presentation tips in this book are practical enough and can generally be applied to any kind of presentations. Whether it be a business meeting, a public presentation or internal presentation, a class presentation, or a conference.

Chapter 1: Have the Tools Ready, Know How to Use Them

"Accept yourself, your strengths, your weaknesses, your truths, and know what tools you have to fulfill your purpose."

- Steve Maraboli

Learn to Set Up a Projector and PC for Business Meetings and Presentations

It is vital for professionals to know how to handle presentation devices appropriately. Knowing this will help you achieve the goal of getting things done quickly and efficiently while presenting.

Regardless of whether a projector, PC, or other presentation equipment has been set up ahead of time for you, you will have to check before your presentation to avoid malfunction during the presentation. This will guarantee that everything works appropriately, and you'll know what to do in the event of a breakdown during the presentation.

With a proper setup and testing, everybody will see your presentation as you have planned it.

The following are tools and devices you should be familiar with before your presentation.

- PC

- Spare batteries

- Extension cords

- Audio and video cables

- Projector and remote control

- Screwdrivers and small pliers

- Power Cords and power adapters

- Copy of your presentation on the PC hard drive

- The right number of copies of handouts for your presentation

- Copies of the presentation on removable media and extra blank media

To ensure that your presentation goes as planned from a technical standpoint, two things to consider having personally and showing up to a conference with include:

- Presentation remote

- Equipment to connect your PC to the projector

Basically, the remote needs to be reliable and compatible with your PC. And only you can be sure of the sort of output your PC needs. These are decent investments, especially if you play a role in your company that requires doing regular business meetings and presentations.

There are other things to take note of to guarantee that you are set up to manage the technical aspects of your presentation. It is common to for the following to happen.

1. Know how to "send the image to a projector." It is shocking to note how many individuals don't know how to do this. Not all PCs do this automatically, and it's even more confusing on a Mac.

2. Driving a projector consumes power. It is therefore essential to confirm that there's an electric socket somewhere nearby to connect your PC to. This will help you avoid draining

your battery during the presentation

3. Turn your screensaver off. Leaving it on is one of the most irritating things to do as the screensaver settings sometimes interfere with the original settings of the projector display.

4. Turn your notifications off. It's distracting for your audience to see notifications popping up from your mail, Facebook, Twitter, or Skype during a meeting.

5. Beware of resolution problems that may arise, especially if you have a PC that is not configured to adjust its resolution to cope with a projector.

6. Keeping a duplicate of your slides in a USB storage device helps. The worst case would be that you have to borrow a PC from the previous speaker. While a cloud storage like Dropbox is alright, it is not advisable because it requires a connection to the internet.

7. Checking the setup in advance helps to eliminate a considerable number of potential issues.

Step-by-Step Instructions to Set up a PC and Projector for Presentations

Presentation software like Microsoft PowerPoint ensures visual dynamism to your meetings and presentations, and the most ideal approach to making your audience know what you're talking about is to use a digital projector to display your slides on a screen. Most modern PCs and an increasing number of tablets have the capacity to interface with a projector due to the presence of a built-in Video Graphics Adapter (VGA) or High Definition Multimedia Interface (HDMI) video output.

1. Before you attempt making any connections, ensure the PC and projector are turned off.

2. Connect the PC and projector using a VGA, DVI, or HDMI video cable, depending on what your PC uses. Merely slot opposite ends of the cable into the projector's "In" port and the PC's external monitor port.

3. Ensure a tight and safe connection of the two ends to avoid a blank screen or an intermittent display. If required, use the right adapter to connect your PC or tablet to the projector.

4. If you have a mouse for remote control, connect the cable to your PC's mouse/USB port, but if your projector uses a wireless remote, ensure it is set up accurately to receive

and send signal.

5. Press the "Input" or "Source" button on your projector corresponding to the video input you use. Different projectors have their own instruction. You may need to press this button several times on some, while you may have to select the right option from a menu on others

6. If the video display does not appear on the projector, you may have to activate it by pressing the key combination on the projector. This usually requires that you hold down the "Function" key together with a specific F-key. You'll generally need to find a key with the picture of a monitor or a text label such as "LCD," "CRT" or "VGA."

7. To ensure that the sound effects of your presentation are felt, connect the projector's sound cable to the PC's "Line Out" and the projector's "Audio In." Ensure that you fix these connections tightly. Speakers or other sound systems can be plugged into your PC's output if the available projector does not have sound input. You may not need an audio cable if the projector and PC support HDMI because HDMI carries both audio and video. In that case, this step can be skipped.

8. Double check the connections to ensure an appropriate connection, and switch on the PC and projector.

When You're Using a Microphone

We've all been at meetings and presentations where the speaker either speaks extremely low or extremely loudly, or continuously hits the mic too loud or drops the mic with a thud leaving everyone's ears ringing.

A mic is expected to amplify your voice and not replace its articulation. It helps make your voice loud so that you can connect with your audience and establish your authority as a speaker. Mics don't make a dull voice fascinating

As a speaker, you can lose natural vocal articulation under the weight of presenting to an audience. However, as you practice different things, be conscious of maintaining your natural voice, and guard against it.

Do a sound check.

There are situations where a sound system specialist sets up the sound equipment and controls the level while you speak. The specialist can be relied upon in this case to set the sound levels according to the room and audience size. In some situations, however, the sound system may just be set up by the specialist, who then leaves the rest to you to do the sound check.

It is possible for you not to have access to a sound system specialist. In this case, you will have to set up the sound system yourself following specific instructions. Keep the instructions close to you and be careful with the sound testing ensure that it's working appropriately.

Regardless of the situation, ensure you go for the rehearsal early, so that you can do a sound check yourself. Your experience using a mic shouldn't tempt you to skip it, as every room and setup comes with different requirements and potential issues.

Get someone to go around the room to test the sound quality and volume. When you are sure of the sound level in the room, increase the volume slightly to make up for the mumblings and rustlings of the real audience.

"Make sure that you always have the right tools for the job. It's no use trying to eat a steak with a teaspoon, and a straw."

- Anthony T. Hincks

Know How the Microphone Works.

Evident as it might appear, be aware of when a mic is on, off, or on standby. Be familiar with the different modes. You would surely not be happy to get off to a fantastic start, only to find that the mic is off. Nor do you want to be heard saying comments that were intended to be private. Switch to the proper mode before and after speaking.

The Lavaliere Mic - Placement is Critical.

The lavaliere mic is the mic which clips to the speaker's outfit. It's therefore important to dress in an outfit that has a lapel or tie, or a suit or blouse with an open front. These are important so that the mic can be easily fastened to you.

The lavaliere mic comes in different forms. It can either be wired or wireless. The wireless form is the most popular form. It comes with a transmitter pack expected to be attached near your waist at the back of your outfit. This requires an additional style demand of wearing a belt to hold the transmitter in place or an outfit with a pocket deep enough to house the transmitter.

The positioning of the mic should be about eight to ten inches below the chin at the center chest region. Ensure that you don't have dressing accessories like jewelry and strands of hair in the way, as the mic will amplify and transmit any small rustle caused by them.

The Lectern Mike - Positioning is Critical.

When using a microphone on a platform or stand, ensure you put yourself at the best possible distance. All sound equipment comes with different requirements. You should therefore ensure that you know the position required by the mic to precisely capture and transmit your voice. When you find this position, talk over and across the mic to test the receptiveness.

Stand with Good Posture.

The vocal cavity needs breath and space to create sound. You can only empower your voice by standing upright, with your head aligned to your spine. This enhances your voice quality and adds to the efficiency of the mic.

You put your voice at a biomechanical disadvantage if you are bent or hunched, as there is a higher tendency for the sound waves produced by your vocal cavity to bounce off your throat rather than come out smoothly towards the audience as you speak. The same applies when your neck is bent or twisted.

Throaty tension should be avoided by coughing out and drinking water several minutes before your presentation. This helps you warm up your voice.

Don't Crowd the Mic.

Crowding simply means "getting too close." Most people often do this, thereby distorting their posture and voice in the process. The mic is designed to transmit any voice that flows over it, therefore getting too close to it means that every sound from your breath, hiss of words, and snap of jaw, will be amplified. This can create annoying noises which may cause the audience to tune out after enduring one or two of such in a presentation session.

Aim your voice directly at the mic, but don't get too close to the mic. This means you'll lean less into the podium. And when using a handheld mic, ensure that your voice follows the direction of the mic. If your head moves, your mic moves, and if your mic moves, your head moves.

Your objective in communication is always to reach your audience. Everything you incorporate into delivering your presentation aims to accomplish that objective. A microphone is only a tool that transmits what you deliver into it. It doesn't turn a poor delivery into a good one, it only amplifies it.

Never Tap On or Blow into a Mic

Most people tap the mic or blow air into it to test if the mic is working. Rather than trying this terrible way to test if a mic is working, say something irrelevant or make noise into it. If you have a technician on ground, make eye contact to let them know you are ready, especially if you are the first presenter.

Never Drop the Mic

Regardless of how great your presentation was, never consider dropping the mic; it can only damage the mic and the setup behind it. Gently put down the mic, or hand it over to the moderator or next speaker.

…Keep in Mind

- Always go through your presentation to ensure it is what you want it to look like, and that the sound (if used) works correctly and is at an acceptable level.

- You might think about having a backup battery in the event of a power outage

- If you have no idea how the room you'll be presenting in is, ensure that all relevant information is on the upper half of the slide so that everyone on every row will be able to see the whole slide.

- Have your presentation stored on an external media and in the cloud and prepare to present it on a PC different from the one you brought. This means that you've prepared to present on a PC with a different operating system other than yours.

- Perform a sound check before you start your

presentation if microphones are provided. Learn to use the microphone.

Know how to use the presentation devices. Nothing looks worse than a presenter that cannot use the equipment.

"It's best to have your tools with you. If you don't, you're apt to find something you didn't expect and get discouraged."

- Stephen King

Chapter 2. Dress for Success

"Dress yourself to define yourself.

- Debasish Mridha

How to Dress for a Presentation

The cliché "first impressions last long" never really gets old in a business setting. This is important in making a great presentation, and every great presenter knows it. Your audience won't judge your presentation on what you present and how you present it alone; how you appear from the start will sometimes influence their judgment.

55% of people's impression of you depends on what you look like. By nature, humans are always quick to form an opinion of others, leading to hasty generalizations. As if that isn't abnormal enough, we develop these opinions based on several shocking and arbitrary factors, like what a person chooses to wear.

As the presenter, it is vital to get your audience to take notice of you and judge you right from the start. You will have the needed effect on them if you get your look right. But what exactly should you consider before choosing an outfit? And what outfit exactly should you wear to win your audience over? Below are tips and tricks on dressing to make your presentation great.

1. Know your Audience

This is one of the principal standards in dressing for a presentation or business meeting. The people and environment in which you will present go a long way in determining the kind of outfit to wear. Different settings and organizations call for different styles of dress, but as a rule of thumb, dress well and slightly better than most of your audience.

While it isn't necessary that you wear designer clothing, sticking to black, navy blue, or grey business suit is usually the best for both men and women. However, ensure they are tailored to fit, high quality, and clean.

2. Your Environment Should Determine Your Outfit

Presenters find it challenging to decide on which outfit to wear because a number of workplaces accept business-casual wears. Stick with the basic rules when in doubt, and never wear excessively loud colors and prints.

As a man, choose a clean and pressed shirt with a sports coat and tie if your audience are people who prefer business casual wears. As a woman, you can select a dressy slack and blazer. However, choose a conservative and moderate outfit if you expect management level people who prefer such dress styles as your audience.

3. Be Comfortably Dressed

Body language is vital in the successful delivery of your presentation. If you wear tight and restrictive clothes, they will negatively affect the delivery of your presentation, and you may end up fidgeting or send signals that show that you are not comfortable.

You want your audience to see a dynamic and engaging presenter. It is therefore best for you to wear clothes that will enable you to move around and send the right non-verbal cues. Also, women should choose wedges or low-heeled shoes over high heels.

4. Don't Miss Little Details

Apart from choosing the right style, always ensure that you're in tune with other little details, like ensuring that your jacket or shirt sleeves are not covering your hands, ensuring that a button isn't missing on your shirt especially in a conspicuous area, ensuring that your outfit doesn't have loose threads or stains, ensuring that your shoes are solid-colored and well-polished, and ensuring that your jewelry and makeup are kept to the bare minimum

Choose the style that makes your audience pay attention to your presentation rather than your outfit. Wear a dark suit on a lighter shirt or blouse. If you are a woman, wear a scarf, especially if it has a bit of red in it.

5. Grooming

Your hair really does make a difference, although it appears to be an insignificant part of your general look. It is essential as a man to trim your hair and beard and ensure that you are clean shaven. If you can't be shaven, brush the hair and keep it short. Your good looks will not impress anyone if you're sporting a two-day stubble. It projects a less professional image. As a woman, your hair should be tied up in a bun or pony-tail to keep it away from your face.

Keep your nails and teeth well-maintained. Your nails should be painted with a natural color, and not matching your outfit. Keep your makeup natural and clean. Having too much color can be distracting.

6. Body Modifications

Every tattoo must be covered either with makeup, clothing, or shoes, depending on its location. The only type of piercings permitted is the single hole in each ear. Other piercings should either be removed or covered. Your audience might still be able to see the scar from your nose piercing (if you ever had one), so think wisely before you do something. Men should not have any visible piercings.

Building Your Professional Wardrobe

Invest your money in great outfits because they last longer and are timeless

Before shopping. Glance through your current wardrobe and look for pieces that are suited for presentation, then shop for "fillers." For example, if you find a nice pair of pants in your wardrobe that just needs a nice belt, buy the belt. This way, you spend smart rather than spending on what you already have.

Shop smart. Before you buy an outfit, think in advance, look for where it is sold, seek the help of a sales representative, and buy versatile pieces

Buy the essentials. As a woman, you should have black pencil skirts, wide-leg trousers (in black, tan or), a white blouse, an elegant handbag, and black pumps. As a man, you should have button-up shirts, a dark and light pair of slacks, dark dress shoes, and a simple belt.

"I think everybody's got a presentation. Everybody looks a certain way because they want to convey a certain image. You look a certain way because you want people to listen to you in a certain way."

- Marilyn Manson

For Women

Suits. Pants or skirt with a matching jacket. The best material to have is pure wool or a wool blend. Black, navy, and charcoal gray are all acceptable colors, while patterns should be muted if present.

Shirts. The best material for your shirt is cotton or cotton blend. It is more professional to use long-sleeved shirts rather than short-sleeved shirts. Stay away from low neckline.

Blouses. Tops can be turtlenecks, button-ups, shells, or fashion blouses. Keep the colors neutral, and don't wear loud patterns or colors. Ensure that whatever you wear covers you.

Skirts. Should be modest in length and not shorter than 2 inches above knee level. When you sit, the skirt should still cover your thighs. Also, ensure that the skirt is suitable for walking and climbing stairs. It can be long but should not be flowing. It should be fitting but not clingy, and short slits are appropriate.

Jewelry. Modest necklace, a ring, and post earrings are acceptable. It is inappropriate to use loud and noisy necklaces, rings on every finger, and dangling earrings. Broaches are acceptable on the jacket as they add color to it.

Shoes. Must be clean, polished, and comfortable with heels below two inches. Closed toe pumps are preferable to open-toed shoes.

Socks/Hosiery. Should cover your ankles or reach mid-calf region and must match the shoes and slacks color. Hosiery must be plain or neutral colored and worn with skirts. Exposing skin due to no hosiery or short socks is unprofessional.

Accessories. Handbags, scarves, and belts should match your outfit. Extras should be kept at a minimum.

For Men

Suits. Pants with a matching jacket. The best material to have is pure wool or a wool blend. Black, navy, and charcoal gray are all acceptable colors, while patterns should be muted if present.

Shirts. The best material for your shirt is cotton or cotton blend. It is more professional to wear long-sleeved shirts rather than short-sleeved shirts.

Jewelry. Modest and kept to a minimum. Only wedding bands and a watch is allowed. Watches should be conservative and not flashy. Earrings and bracelets are unprofessional

Ties. Buy quality ties. It should not go below the top of your belt buckle. It is more professional to use a 100% silk tie, which are stain resistant and do not wrinkle. Ensure that you can knot a tie correctly or have someone help you. It is meant to complement your suit and enhance your appearance and not overshadow your outfit. The patterns could either be a diagonal stripe or geometric, or small to medium dotted, or solid.

Shoes. May or may not have shoelaces. The best material is leather.

Socks. Should cover your ankles or reach mid-calf region and must match the shoes and slacks color. Exposing skin due to short socks is unprofessional.

Accessories. Should be kept to a minimum. Vests, cuff links, and ties should match the rest of your outfit, but don't wear all at once.

…Keep in Mind

Research has revealed that first impressions are formed in a split second. Therefore, your audience paints a clear picture of you and your company way before your presentation starts. The goal is to look the best you can because you may be meeting new clients or partners

So, focus on dressing well, and make every second count. Keep it business and professional. Don't experiment with new clothes or radical colors; the way you dress represents you and your company.

Wear deodorant, appropriate jewelry, and natural looking makeup. Brush your teeth and hair, and trim and polish your nails. Don't wear overpowering cologne or perfume and trendy clothes. Don't try out elaborate hairstyles.

If you question an item, don't wear it. Keep it neutral, keep it covered, keep it classy, keep it smart.

"The way that people dress makes them part of an army, dressed in their own uniform, determined to do something."

- Suzy Menkes

Chapter 3. Stay Focused, Have a Plan and Follow It

"The biggest challenge is to stay focused. It's to have the discipline when there are so many competing things."

- Alexa Hirschfeld

Staying Focused and Keeping Your Audience Focused on Your Presentation

It's common today to see people give boring presentations in the business world, but that is tantamount to mental abuse. Also, it's a loss if your content is not presented in a way that wins the sustained attention of your audience, regardless of the value in the content.

Some practical tips to stay focused and deliver engaging presentations that will keep your audience focused on your message include:

1. Stay on Topic

Be sure to make your audience know your goal within the first two minutes of your meeting. Ensure that they understand the value the information you are presenting will bring to them. Within these two minutes, your agenda should be stated. Stick to it, and this way, they can all stay focused in anticipation of a productive and informative presentation session.

2. Stick to Time

Gone are the days of two-hour meetings and presentations. You don't expect people just to focus while sitting at a PC - it's just too long. You shouldn't spend more time than expected at your session. If possible, make it shorter. It is more productive to have a shorter presentation session with points that are direct. If it's too long, people will zone out, and allow interruptions by colleagues, e-mails, and web ads.

3. Be Conscious of the 10-Minute Rule.

Most presenters seem to forget that attention fades after about 10 minutes. They continue rambling on for minute upon minute, going from one mind-numbing slide to the other, insensitive of the effect it's having on the audience.

When creating your presentation, have a strategy to stimulate some audience interaction every 10 minutes. Asking a good question, telling a short story, showing a short video, or making the audience analyze a chart are ideas that can generate the needed change in atmosphere.

4. Use Images.

When humans hear or read information, only 10% of it is remembered after three days. However, if pictures are added, more than 65% of this information will be remembered. This is because vision trumps all other senses.

In preparing your presentation, endeavor to reduce the number of text-based slides because they are ineffective in sustaining audience-focus. Get affordable and quality images to spice up your presentation. Images are useful in aiding memory. They can be obtained from sites such as iStock photo, Pixabay, Fotolia, and Shutter Stock.

5. Don't Neglect the Use of Graphs, Figures, and Charts

Graphs and figures are appealing visual approaches to pass the information on some of your slides. PowerPoint has a fantastic SmartArt feature that gives you the option of different diagrams to pass your message. Figures and charts to translate your numerical data can be created and imported from Microsoft Excel. Graphs, pictures, and maps help energize your talk

6. Respect the Audience

Switching the spotlight from yourself to the audience is the best way to liven up the audience. A statement like, "The talent in this room is immense. I urge you to share your ideas on the topic with others so that we can learn from each other," is simple enough to place the limelight on them.

7. Use Other Options Apart from Lecturing

When delivering a presentation, there are practical alternatives to use instead of presenting it as a lecture.

For example, animations can be used to map the points on your slide. Do this and watch your audience stay glued to your presentation.

"Your purpose is your identity; focus your energy on great purposes."

- Amit Ray

8. Connect the Dots for People.

When presenting, help people see how your slides flow into each other so that they can understand where you were, and have an idea of the direction in which you are headed. Use pointers such as, "Firstly...", "The second reason is...", "The next point is crucial...", "Remember this...", and "This is important for our company." These transitions help your audience get the message of why they should care, thereby engaging their minds to ask questions such as: "why this?", "so what?", "what's the benefit?", etc. Those who have zoned out will become re-engaged and re-interested in the presentation.

9. Learn to Use Questions

Open-ended questions are valuable during presentations, but difficult to think of on the spot.

During your preparations, draw a collection of such questions that you can choose from in moments when you need them. These questions and comments are useful in keeping the conversation going. Examples of such questions are: "How would you explain it?, "Can you imagine being there?", "Could you please tell me more?", "How would you conclude?", "How did we get here?".

10.   Stay Away from Making the Slides Your Speaking Notes.

Many otherwise intelligent people display slides that should be called "TextPoints" or "PowerTexts" rather than "PowerPoint." These slides are usually dense with texts, and it is incredible how these presenters expect the audience to follow through on listening to them speak and reading the slides. This is the most unforgivable sin a presenter can commit. You are presenting to a professional audience reading to them will mostly insult them as you as implying they do not know how to read or cause them to lose interest.

The visual channel overrides the auditory, and if the information on your slides is too complicated and congested for people to look at or read, then it may be difficult for them to continue listening to you as they will struggle with reading in-between lines of a bullet and completing a slide. It's worse if the speaker just talks without being sensitive to the audience body language.

11. Stay Away from the Graveyard Shift.

Having people listen to us is a privilege that comes with the responsibility to pass our message in a stimulating, engaging, and intellectual way. So, stay away from presenting immediately after lunch if possible, because attention span efficiently reduces any time after 11:00 am. The best time of the day for maximum attention is between 7:00 am, and 11:00 am

...Keep in Mind

To make your presentation effective, the audience must be engaged. To accomplish that objective, you need to plan and prepare for audience-presenter interactions using slides with animations, images, and fewer text. Spend time thinking about the audience, what value they can get from what you have to offer, and how to make it easy for them. An audience-focused presentation is essential.

Presentations skills are worthy of obsessive study. It is therefore advantageous to devote some time to improving yours. This is a fantastic and smart move for anyone in the business of attending meetings and presentations to communicate key company messages.

Multitasking and jumping around will lose everyone in the meeting.

"A clear vision backed by definite plans, give you a tremendous feeling of confidence and personal power" – Brian Tracy.

Chapter 4. Know When to Cut a Topic Off and How

"If you want a happy ending, that depends, of course, on where you stop your story." - Orson Welles

Right Ways to End Your Presentation

As fuel begins to run down in a car, it sputters to a sudden stop. Have you noticed this is the same way many speakers end their presentation? As if they became weary of thinking. Then they use lines such as, "Erm, looks like that's about all I have," "looks like the time is up," "that should be it, THE END."

Hopefully, you aren't one of the presenters who end their presentations with these common but entirely ineffective endings, and if you are, this chapter addresses the right way to end your presentation.

Closing your presentation comes with its own challenges. Strange situations come up, like running out of time, taking several challenging questions, or failing to get your ideas accepted. No matter how good or bad your presentation is, your ability to influence the audience will be significantly detracted by a terrible ending.

The last chance you have to send home the value of your information is the closing stage of your presentation. It leaves a lasting impression that your audience has of you and the company you represent.

Don't leave the last 30 seconds of your presentation to chance. Below are some powerful and killer ideas to make your listeners sit up and stay focused listening to your final statement as your presentation enters its closing stages.

A Surprising Fact.

Rather than end your presentation by rehashing the presentation, decide to motivate your audience by sharing a surprising fact. While your audience's attention may have waned by the end of your presentation, a surprising fact is sure to re-engage the audience's attention.

A List of Rolling Credits.

The opportunity to publicly thank people who helped you prepare a fantastic presentation may just be at that all-important business meeting. PowerPoint's credits feature helps make this easy. It is sure to be noticed because it's an unusual thing to do.

A Cartoon.

Ending your presentation with a cartoon is a brilliant idea because it engages the audience combining visual, humorous, and metaphoric elements. Consider using a relevant cartoon to end your presentation and drive home your message.

A Provocative Question.

Questions stimulate our neocortex. Therefore, it is a sure way to gain attention. Our brain has become configured to use questions to challenge the existing process. The audience is generally stimulated to think of an answer once you choose to ask a question. A rhetorical or provocative question does the job better than an ordinary question, and more engaging is a question relating to sensitive areas.

A Tweet Line.

It sends home the central message of your presentation in Twitter-sized attention span. Think about how you can make a memorable statement message with two sentences, or 140 characters. Ask yourself if it's tweet-worthy after you've crafted it in your subconscious. Ensure that the line accurately condenses what your message is about and that it represents your authentic voice. Make it an opportunity to genuinely communicate a vital message, rather than just be an effort to impress. This approach is an attention magnet.

The Rule of Three.

Think: "Just do it," "location, location, location," "make it real," "start something now," "let's do this," "love your life," "be a team," "stand for justice', etc. These are memorable patterns of three words, and that's basically what the rule of three stands for. It's usually a three-word slogan that gets registered in the hearts of your audience at the end of the presentation. When they remember you or your presentation, they remember the words and easily remember the information or value your presentation afforded them.

"There is no real ending. It's just the place where you stop the story."

- Frank Herbert

An Unusual Quote.

This is a relatively easy but powerful approach to end your presentation. It will be more effective if it's a quote that isn't heard too often that it's become a cliché. It's even more effective when it's personalized to resonate with the audience. The quote must be relevant to the message you are passing if you want to drive home the point.

A Touch of Humility.

If you are more affluent or higher up in rank than most of your audience, there's a high possibility that you have made a compelling case or statement in your presentation that flashes your achievements and opinions. However, regardless of the undertone your presentation relays, ending it with a touch of humility adds immense value to your presentation.

A Running Clock.

If the message you're delivering is time-sensitive, and you want your listeners to move along with you as quickly as possible, having a background slide with a running clock is a great approach. This way, your audience knows you're sticking with time and, unconsciously, they are focused on not missing out of the value you are adding as the countdown timer runs out.

A Powerful Visual.

A large portion of human brain power is committed to processing visual images. It's also the way we communicate and share information. We understand the universe by images, pictures, and videos. Utilize this power by ending your presentation with a mind-blowing visual relating to the take-home from your core message. The image stands as a visual metaphor, enabling your audience to remember the message long after.

A Return to Your Opening.

This is another easy way out of the "signing off" problem that most presenters face. A standard piece of advice on ending your presentation is to refer to the hook you started your presentation with. This can be a reaffirmation of your presentation title, or the title of the conference at which you're speaking, or a conclusion of a story you started the presentation with, or an answer to the question you posed at the beginning. It's a book-end closure, and you can't go wrong with it.

One More Thing.

Use the line "one more thing" to add richness and dynamism as you end your presentation. Steve Jobs was known to conclude his presentations with this famous line. It's the icing on the cake. Those words mentally prepare people to move on. Use it with care and only when you really mean it.

Something More Exciting and Original.

This is a personal favorite. You could conclude your presentation with a related statement or idea, or question suggested by the presentation and broadens the discussion. It should get people thinking or give them something to talk about over the tea break, lunch, and into the next few weeks

Turn Your Audience Loose on the Action.

Turning the audience loose on the action is another great way to end a presentation. Give them an opportunity to move or do something, after all you've literally asked them to sit passively for 20 minutes or more. Whatever you choose to turn them on to should be related to what your presentation is all about. It should be specific and straightforward. Get them to add up three numbers, get them to suggest a fact to each other, get them to repeat the vision statement to each other in turn, get them to turn to each other and pledge to make a healthy living choice, etc. As long as it resonates with your presentation's core message.

The Questioner Plant.

If you are presenting in a business meeting, there is a high chance of getting myriad questions. However, if you're afraid of not getting any questions, arrange for a friend to ask one in the audience. If you fear silence, the "plant" is an excellent way to get the questions rolling in.

If you want to answer more questions, stay away from asking, "Are there any more questions?" Instead ask, "What other questions can I answer?" or. "What questions do you have?" Do not make it the duty of a slide to ask a question if you really want to engage in questions. It suggests that you fear questions.

Get over yourself, it's someone else's turn to speak. Let them speak to your presentation, after all you've had the floor for 45 minutes. If you are terrified of answering questions, you can turn it into a strength by sharing your fear and saying, "Little questions at presentations like this scare me, but since I have more knowledgeable people in the audience, I'd be happy with the idea of agreeing to turn the answers over to anyone who is better positioned than I am to answer the question". You can also offer to answer further questions after the meeting.

Get a Talkback from the Audience.

The theatre has a fantastic way of doing this. Some groups beckon the audience to share their thoughts to the stage crew, director, actors, or any other person available. It's a question and answer session, therapy session, and focus group discussion all rolled up into one, with the goal of critiquing the movie or play and ideas behind the acts. You can choose this approach if you are really grounded in the subject you are talking on. This is a risky move because you are at the mercy or terrible critics in the audience who just want to bloviate and rant. However, this can help you relay some points which aren't easily understood. If you have a moderator on ground, then this person can help moderate the talkback.

Thank You.

Saying "thank you" is the simplest way to conclude a presentation, particularly after you've finished the content part. It is unexceptional, unambiguous, and has the virtue of being understood individually. Saying "thank you" remains my go-to recommendation to tell the audience that it's time to leave.

You are not thanking the audience for their time, but rather for participating and offering feedbacks or comments. You should honestly thank them for their passion about the subject matter if the meeting was contentious.

"Thank you" is pure, neat, simple, and gets the job done. You can choose to give out your contact information if you are okay with it.

...Keep in Mind

It is crucial for you to nail your presentation in the last minute regardless of the situations leading up till the end. A dull closure will fundamentally take away your last opportunity to impress and influence your audience, so don't leave the closing to chance.

Your ending should be positive and forward-focused. It should make people remember what they have accomplished or learned even if disagreements ensued. Until you are ready to end, do not say "in conclusion" or "in closing." A brisk "thank you" is a great idea for a perfect closure. However, ensure that your main message or a call to action is reinforced just before the "thank you."

There are plenty of great ways to end a presentation. Get to work, discard that "Any Questions" slide, take time to plan the ending of your next meeting or presentation so that you can end with finesse regardless of what happens.

"Most people remember the ending of the book more than the beginning and the middle."

- Bernard Hopkins

Chapter 5. Don't Break the Fourth Wall

"A positive attitude causes a chain reaction of positive thoughts, events, and outcomes. It is a catalyst, and it sparks extraordinary results."

- Wade Boggs

The Right Attitude to Delivering an Effective Presentation

Everyone who is charged with the responsibility of making a presentation should be ready to be put on public display. The audience not only listens to your idea, but also respond to your voice and body language. As much as you need a well-written and structured presentation to make an impact, you also need to have a lively, flexible, and exciting delivery. You need to add energy and style when presenting.

If you were the audience for your presentation, what would:

- win your attention?

- charge your confidence?

- ignite your creative ability?

- build up your understanding?

- Now think about ways to encourage these things.

To be an effective presenter, you must be energetic, flexible, optimistic, and enthusiastic. You need the right attitude to turn your presentation into an imaginative public delivery.

1. Practice

You'll be more capable and better positioned to inspire your audience's confidence and trust in your presentation if you appear comfortable with what you are presenting. Regular practice by reading the material to yourself, standing in a room and delivering to the walls, talking to a set of cutleries on the dining table, etc. can help you be better ready. This will get you used to filling a room with your own voice, and make you familiar with the phrases and words in the presentation.

Know how well your voice can be heard by playing around with different volumes. Most importantly, get used to the main idea of your presentation and explore how the individual elements fit into each other. With this, you will be able to focus on your objectives and stay away from distractions when D-Day comes.

To learn or to read? Should you present entirely from memory or read out your presentation from detailed notes? Each has its own advantages and disadvantages, so find a way of balancing the two approaches.

Learning. This can be fun until you lose your way or become distracted. It is therefore better to have some form of notes to keep you in line. There is a tendency to lose energy and sense of enthusiasm if you have over-learned your notes. Be confident and work towards being spontaneous

Reading. This makes you focus solely on your notes, thereby losing touch with your audience. Your voice can be reduced to a monotone when reading, eliminating energy, flair, and enthusiasm from your delivery. Reading tends to focus your thoughts on your notes, thus losing contact with your audience. It's much more engaging to directly address your audience even as you read, rather than just read directly.

In balancing the two, try making notes to support your style of presentation. Notes such as index cards can be read at a glance as visual prompts to guide you while presenting. Each vital point can be on each card, with each idea carrying critical supporting details for each point. To avoid the cards falling out of order, they can be held together with a piece of string or a tag.

2. Assert Yourself

There is a thin line between assertiveness and aggressiveness. A good presenter ought to be assertive and self-assured, not aggressive or forceful. The two crucial Ps involved in being an assertive presenter include posture and presence

Posture. Different postures portray different moods.

Rather than create a relaxed and active atmosphere with your posture, a still, upright, and formal posture will create a very different one. Your presentation must be supported by a matching physical behavior. Make deliberate choices about your preferred physical styles. Stick with being formal, and in doing so, it is vital to consistently always sport a posture that shows you are confident.

Presence. Having the confidence to fill and use the space in front of your audience is one quality of being a great presenter. Be unapologetic for filling and using the space. Hiding behind the lectern or desk are signs of physical apologies. The only time you must apologize is when circumstances demand. You must be confident about what you have to tell the audience if you want them to be assured of getting something interesting and valuable from you. If they haven't settled down before you start your presentation, don't be afraid to wait for them or ask for quiet.

3. Make Contact with Your Audience

It's usually challenging for most presenters to connect with their audience, and this usually results from being unable to read their body language. Audience interest is maintained and encouraged when a presenter can make contact with them. They will believe that you are indeed happy and looking forward to telling them more things. Eye contact, verbal contact, gestures, and language usage are ways in which contact can be established with your audience.

Eye contact. An audience can feel awkward if they are denied eye to eye connection with the presenter, and this is because they see it as the most critical aspect of everyday communication. You give your audience a feeling of involvement in your presentation if you make eye contact with them, and your presentation's core objective gets to them on a personal level by doing this.

Regardless of how big the room is, ensure that everyone gets their share of eye contact by consistently shifting your focus around the room. This doesn't make you look anxious. Instead, it gets many people involved in your presentation.

Try looking at their foreheads if making eye contact with a large audience is difficult. People sitting around them will interpret this as you giving eye contact to them. Never should you look at the floor or ceiling, it sends a message of rudeness or boredom to the audience. Never turn your back on the audience.

Verbal contact. Starting your presentation by speaking with your audience is a way to acknowledge and connect with them. Ask if they can hear you or see your presentation clearly from their end of the room. Ask rhetorical questions during your presentation like, "How do we prove this" or, "So, how did I know this?" Then answer the questions yourself. Give the audience a chance to ask questions and make contributions at the end of your presentation.

Questions are a surefire way of connecting with your audience verbally, as it engages their mind in a more stimulating way, beyond them just sitting and listening to you talk. If your audience is verbally drawn in with clear and focused questions, they will be encouraged and feel like a massive part of your presentation.

Gesture. Use arms and hands in conversations to describe events or add emphasis. You'll look awkward as a presenter if you keep your hands firmly rooted at your sides or in your pockets. In a presentation, gestures can be used to welcome your audience, emphasize your points, or indicate an ending. Endeavor to make use of gestures which extend away from your body to your audience. This helps to have the audience focus on your presentation.

Always guide against using your gesticulations to distract the audience from the content of your presentation. Ensure that your gestures are precise and controlled, as excessive gesticulations will be seen as nervousness and lack of focus. Gesticulations help your audience listen to you and understand your presentation better.

Language. The use of languages that resonates with your audience is vital in creating and sustaining a relationship with them. The use of "we" in your presentation helps your audience connect with you. For example, when you ask questions, say, "How can we learn from this?" or, "Where do we go from here?"

and when using ordinary statements, say "If we look at this picture closely," Your choice of language is meant to welcome and involve your audience throughout your presentation, not make them lose interest.

"If you want to connect, you must let them reflect."

- Darren Lacroix

Never turn your back. This is by far the largest faux pas many presenters do, this is how you break the 4th wall with your audience. You lose eye contact with your audience, they can no longer follow your body language thereby breaking the hold you had them under with your dynamic presentation.

If you're using computer aid, have your computer screen facing you as you, while you continue to face the audience. You can always tell exactly what's on the presentation screen screen just by looking at your computer screen. This style of presentation also applies to physical presentations like white board or flip chart.

4. Use Your Voice

Your voice can be used to connect with your audience in different ways. It is a flexible and powerful tool. The use of your voice during a presentation should vary in volume, pitch, and pace.

Volume. Ensure that your voice is loud and audible enough to be heard by your audience. If you speak too loudly or quietly, it can be difficult for your audience to hear you and follow your presentation. When people speak in regular everyday conversations, they tend to adjust their volume in response to certain situations. For example, when apologizing, they speak softly, but loudly when giving instructions. Use these beautiful and dynamic volume changes to add flair and energy to your presentation. A loud exclamation can make your audience sit up, while a conspiratorial whisper can draw them in.

Pitch. Like volume, your voice pitch also varies in everyday conversation. When presenting, it is important to leverage this strength to connect with your audience. For example, your pitch will be reduced when you want to sound severe but will be raised when asking a question.

Pace. The speed of your delivery plays an immense role in ensuring that your audience follows your presentation. Your audience will find it difficult to follow you if you speak too slowly or too quickly. Try adjusting the pace of your delivery to add life to your presentation. A slightly slower section might pass the message of caution or emphasis, while a slightly faster delivery can mean optimism or enthusiasm.

When practicing your presentation, play around with

volume, pitch, and pace to find different ways of passing the message a sentence is meant to pass. Familiarize yourself with your preferred voice ranges to add emphasis, enthusiasm, and energy to your presentation's core message.

5. Breathe

Steady and deep breaths should be used in presentations. Anxiety makes your breathing fast and shallow, leading to poor voice quality and an inability to speak clearly for an extended period of time. Before commencing your presentation, attempt a few deep breaths, and make conscious efforts to slow down your breaths and take in more air with each inhalation. While presenting, try using pauses between sections or after questions to ensure comfortable breathing patterns. If your breathing becomes uncomfortable, don't be afraid of slowing down the pace of your presentation.

6. Drink

Having some liquid on hand is a good idea if you are speaking for a long time, as it will help quench your thirst. Before you go on, ensure you drink a cup of warm tea or water to relax your throat and voice, but never drink anything ice-cold because it will constrict your voice.

...A Note about Humor

Make use of humor only if you know it will work. It needs to be confident and relaxed. If humor is poorly used, it will make the presentation awkward and heighten your sense of anxiety. Use humor if you can and only when you feel it is appropriate.

...Keep in Mind

Consistently explore your preferred style, applying any or all of the above recommendations for different impacts and effects. Most importantly, be yourself and avoid any attitude that might offend your audience.

You will impress nobody by trying to perform like a stand-up comedian, and you will pass no message if you aren't deliberate and explicit in how you use your voice and physical actions. Have the right attitude during presentations.

"A director is a general in charge of an army of traitors like any showman. An audience will love you, laugh with you and wait outside your stage door when you're hot and on a roll, but no audience is ever truly friendly. Not for long. Bore 'em or disappoint 'em - even once - and they'll turn on you and tear you to pieces, regardless of who you are or might once have been."

- Richard Stanley

Chapter 6. Start and Finish on Time

"Blessed is the man who, having nothing to say, abstains from giving us wordy evidence of the fact — from calling on us to look through a heap of millet-seed in order to be sure that there is no pearl in it."

— George Eliot

Keeping to Time in Presentations

Time restriction is a natural element of most presentations. It is your responsibility to finish your presentation within the set time limit. Consider this as an agreement between you and your audience. At some presentations, you might be given separate time limits for speaking and questions, while at others, you will be allotted an overall timeslot for both speaking and questions. Keeping to time is a demonstration of regard for your audience. It ensures you deliver an engaged, focused, and effective presentation.

What Goes Wrong?

The two primary reasons time limits are usually

exceeded include:

- There is too much information cramped up into one presentation by the presenter that the time allowed is too little to take it all

- The presentation process of speaking, distributing materials, and using visual aids has simply taken additional, which the presenter hasn't planned for.

Managing the Content

During preparations for your presentation, it is vital to know what can be accomplished within the set time limit. A written essay or report will typically carry and communicate more information than a presentation will. Therefore, manage the amount of information you intend to pass in your presentation. Ensure that it's direct, concise, and focused.

Planning

Prioritizing your information is vital, especially at the early stage of planning for your presentation. During the planning process, set your notes aside and write a simple outline of what you intend to present. The outline should be from a progression of logically structured core points.

Ensure that each of the key points can be expressed in a few words or a basic sentence. If you can't do this, there is every likelihood that you still aren't sure of your presentation's focus or core message. It is important to note that a clear focus increases the chances of delivering an effective and impactful presentation.

After identifying your main points, proceed to support your argument with suitable data. Carefully select each main point's supporting detail. It'll be quite easy for the audience to recollect one or two impactful examples. Less enlightening data will not be as effective.

Lastly, plan a powerful introduction (opening) and conclusion (closure) for your presentation. As discussed in earlier chapters, the information you include in these sections must be effective. Don't leave its essential elements to chance.

Flexibility

The content of your presentation will be hard to adapt and reduce if you have written it as a complete script. To produce a flexible presentation fit to the time allotted, you should adopt a structured plan as stated above. If this means you have to reduce the content of your presentation, reduce it. Your goal is to deliver quality information in the time allotted, not to bore your audience with extended rigid content with little or no relevance.

Managing the Execution

Presenters often run out of time when presenting because they took only a few aspects of their performance into consideration when structuring and rehearsing their presentation. When preparing for how to execute your delivery, you need to include time to:

- settle in front of your audience to set up your notes and visual aids before you start presenting;

- distribute materials at the beginning, within, and when concluding your presentation;

- come up with additional detailed explanations if your audience appears not to understand a particular section of your presentation;

- accommodate any slight unprepared deviations from your content;

- work with your visual aids including changing of slides, annotating images, etc.;

- allow your audience to think between main points;

- accommodate pauses that may come up while you're reviewing your notes;

- respond to questions while presenting and when you've finished (if there's no separate time for questions.

You need to control the delivery of your presentation for it to have the best impact. Give time for the different components of your presentation so that it will not look congested and rushed.

"Some people rehearse to a point where they're robotic, and they sound like they have memorized their presentation and didn't take it to the next level. Going from sounding memorized and canned to sounding natural is a lot of work."

- Nancy Duarte

Planning How to Use Your Time

After writing the content of your presentation, it is essential to map out how you intend it to be delivered. This includes a clear plan of when the materials will be handed out, the precise time you'll explain specific slides, and the point where questions will be taken. This is to make the components of your presentation look more deliberate, in addition to ensuring that such non-spoken sections of the presentation are allotted time. Just like a movie script includes specific directions to remind actors of what to do and when to do it, an efficient presenter will mark such points on the notes of their presentation so that they are altogether incorporated in the final execution.

During rehearsal, don't just run through the words. Try as much as possible to present close to what you want to present on the main day. Only a few aspects of the presentation will be played out if you just run through the words in your head. Try the presentation out in reality in a lecture theatre or seminar room similar to where you'll present on day, so that you can integrate and time all the aspects of the presentation. Time the whole thing. If this means that you have to rehearse loud and pause where you've highlighted a pause or other activities to take place, do it. It's lead to an excellent presentation.

1. Decide your "talk time." Although you know beforehand how long you are expected to talk for, it is impossible to keep to time. Your "talk time" is not the same as the total time allotted for your presentation for two reasons:

- Time needs to be allotted for questions. If this isn't decided by the meeting organizer, then as a rule of thumb you should give this section about 20 to 25% of your presentation time.

- Rehearsals generally take less time than the time for live presentations due to different factors that are probably out of your control. There may be delaying interruptions, you might begin some minutes late, or it might take you more time to get a point across.

So, if thirty minutes is allotted to you as your presentation time, you should take twenty minutes as your talk time, seven minutes for questions, and three minutes for delays and interruptions.

2. Find out how much time you're allotted. This is essential in keeping to time. You may not be able to meet the time limit if you have no idea how long you're given to present. Most presenters are bad judges of time when they are on the platform. Awful judges. You have definitely been at presentations where the presenter presented for 17 minutes instead of 10 minutes, rushing through the final moments of their presentation. This is even after rehearsing their presentation – poor time planning.

You will save yourself time and pain if you do a proper time planning early in the process. If you wait until the end to plan for the timing of your presentation, there's a high chance of realizing that you've prepared too much content and will have to edit your presentation. The pain here is that you've already grown too attached to your material to want to remove any aspect.

3. Prepare a schedule for different sections of

your presentation. During your final rehearsal, highlight the number of minutes each section takes and use that to prepare a time schedule for the different sections. Assuming your presentation is to start at 9am, this is what your schedule will look like:

9.00 - Opening

9.03 - Part 1

9.10 - Part 2

9.15 - Part 3

9.22 - Closing

9.25 – Stop talking

This means that it'll be easy for you to tell during the live presentation if you are keeping to time. You must get used to this timing before the real presentation, because you may not have the head space to calculate whether you're ahead or behind during the live presentation.

4. Write down points to avoid waffling. A live

presentation can exceed the normal time if you waffle. It works like this: you say your point, but the audience doesn't get it, so you make it more explicit, and they still don't get it, and you elaborate some more, and some more, and suddenly you are waffling. This can be avoided if you plan well. During preparations, don't write each point as a bullet point; write them as full sentences that carry the exact message you want to pass. Then start reducing it to keywords or phrases in your notes as you get used to the real messages. You'll find that, even when you see the phrase, you will pass the message in clear terms as you have initially written. This way, you will avoid hard thinking during the presentation itself.

5. Have a clock or timekeeper. Managing time is

difficult if you can't see the time. Always keep track of time by referring to a clock at a visible angle in the room, although you can't assume that every meeting or conference room will have a clock. Having a small but easily readable travel clock is a great idea. This can be placed on the desk or lectern or in front of you on the stage. As an alternative, you can prop up your wristwatch on the desk or lectern before you to avoid looking down at your wrist too often. Ensure that the clock or wristwatch is at a distance where you can read it without your glasses on. Some remotes have a countdown timer that buzzes at specific times before you end your presentation. You are lucky if the meeting or conference organizers plan for this.

6. Begin on time. Most presentations end late merely because they didn't start early, and that's often because of the presenter or meeting organizer's decision to wait for latecomers. It's not possible to have as much time as desired. You should start on time if you're in control. Don't penalize people who made an effort to be early by having to wait for latecomers.

Don't start the presentation with crucial information if you are concerned that latecomers will miss out on it. Rather, start with an engaging and related story leading up to your first main point. Latecomers will arrive when you're telling the story, but if they don't, continue with your presentation.

7. Be ready to adapt. You may still run short of time even if you prepare well ahead of the real presentation. Don't take to talking faster as a way out. Rather, do a mental evaluation of what points or sections you won't elaborate.

If you can, make a mental note of the slide number you want to jump to, key in the number and press "Enter" to jump to the slide. It is more professional to do this than just click through the slide. Your audience doesn't have to know that you did a real-time jumping. Though, do this only if you are confident.

Cutting Time

Despite the fact that you stuck to time when rehearsing for the presentation, it is essential to spare a couple of minutes or for the real presentation, because more time than expected will be taken up by nerves and any interaction with your audience. It is better and safer to prepare to be a little under time to ensure you can address all sections of your presentation and avoid rushing.

After organizing your presentation around your core message and supporting data, reducing the length of your presentation should become easy. Cut out some details or review some of the main points to save a small amount of time. Do not attempt to increase the pace of the delivery; it's amateurish and can have an adverse effect on your intended impact.

Dealing with the 'Mental Clock.'

A number of presenters keep themselves to time by depending on their own mental awareness of time passing. This rarely works in practice unless you are an exceptionally experienced presenter. It is quite common for presenters to think that they have spoken for only 5 minutes when it's much closer to 15 minutes. Never lose track of time.

During your rehearsal, time your delivery and make a note on your script at which point should have reached 5, 10, 15 minutes, etc. Pause for a moment if it looks like you're coming up short on time, and review what you can reasonably accomplish in the last few minutes. No matter how brief, never forget to include a conclusion. This point is very vital for the success of your presentation. It is the opportunity to make a lasting impression on your audience.

…Keep in Mind

In keeping to time, you are required to carefully prioritize the information you include in your presentation. Carefully plan each component of your delivery, from the script, to your use of visual aids, interaction with the audience, questions from the audience, etc. Thoroughly rehearse your presentation so that you have a clear understanding of how each component of the presentation fits and can measure the amount of time to be designated to each component.

During delivery, do not lose focus of time, and be prepared to adjust your presentation to fit the time remaining. The more experienced you become, the better you will be at deciding how much information to be included within a specific timeframe. However, always rehearse your presentation to time, as experience isn't fail-proof.

"My best advice is to not start in PowerPoint. Presentation tools force you to think through information linearly, and you really need to start by thinking of the whole instead of the individual lines."

- Nancy Duarte

Conclusion

"PowerPoint may not be of any use for you in a presentation, but it may liberate you in another way, an artistic way. Who knows."

- David Byrne

We've all sat through an excruciatingly dry, boring, and scripted presentation with nothing to interest us on the screen apart from bullet points with full sentences and lousy clipart. To make it worse, there was no effort on the part of the presenter to keep us interested or help us understand the material. Nothing displayed or said was worth looking at or listening to. We felt like we were in hell, counting down to the closing moments when we could take our leave.

As the presenter, it doesn't have to be that way. You can save your audience.

Let's face it, there's a high chance of your audience listening to what you have to say if they are convinced you are credible, even when it is not about your impressive CV or lengthy intro with your career highlights. You can become that vibrant and effective presenter whose passion and message gets through to each and every member of the audience.

It takes practice. However, with a few practical tips up your sleeve, taking up the challenge will be easy for you. Know how to use the tools, dress well, engage your audience, let them know the goal of the presentation from the start, connect with them so that they can relate what you have to say with your intended goal, and don't waste their time and trust.

Be confident in describing your ideas, and how you want to turn them into reality. In the end, it becomes easy to get the reaction you want, whether it's funding, approval to proceed with an initiative, to change their minds, or simply get agreement and understanding.

BONUS OFFER

Wouldn't it be nice to know when ACR Publishing releases a new book or their books go on
Free promotion? Or new books come out
Check us out at ACRPublishing.com
As a thank you for reading a book by ACR Publishing we would like to offer you the opportunity to receive access to a service that will notify you when a new book is released or other books from ACR Publishing go on sale. If you are someone interested in saving money and learn more from our books simply visit our site!

Look for More Business books

By

ACR PUBLISHING

Please don't forget to leave a Review.